COMPOSER SHOWCASE
HAL LEONARD STUDENT PIANO LIBRARY

Hal Leonard
7777 West Bluemound Road
Milwaukee, WI 53213
Email: info@halleonard.com

Impressions of New York

A JAZZ SONATINA BY MONA REJINO

ISBN 978-1-70513-366-8

HAL•LEONARD®

Copyright © 2021 by HAL LEONARD LLC
International Copyright Secured   All Rights Reserved

No part of this publication may be reproduced in any form or by
any means without the prior written permission of the Publisher.

Visit Hal Leonard Online at
www.halleonard.com

Contact us:
Hal Leonard
7777 West Bluemound Road
Milwaukee, WI 53213
Email: info@halleonard.com

In Europe, contact:
Hal Leonard Europe Limited
42 Wigmore Street
Marylebone, London, W1U 2RN
Email: info@halleonardeurope.com

In Australia, contact:
Hal Leonard Australia Pty. Ltd.
4 Lentara Court
Cheltenham, Victoria, 3192 Australia
Email: info@halleonard.com.au

Preface

Impressions of New York was originally written as a trio, commissioned by the Music Teachers National Association for the 2019 National Conference in Spokane, Washington. Since I am a pianist, it seemed worthwhile to arrange this music for piano so that it could also be performed as a solo work.

Creating interesting melodies, rich harmonies, and adding a touch of jazz has been my goal in writing this composition. *Impressions of New York* explores the sights and sounds one might encounter when visiting this vibrant city. The first movement, *Strolling the Upper West Side*, has a suave, sophisticated feel. You can imagine walking down a tree-lined street in this lovely neighborhood on a beautiful, sunny day. The second movement, *Midnight in Brooklyn*, exudes a slow, sultry mood. Picture yourself sitting in a club late at night as the day winds down, being transformed by the music of a fine jazz musician. The final movement, *Grand Central Station*, has a frenetic pace depicting scores of people rushing through this crowded architectural giant, as they race from one train to another to reach their destination. The third movement is the most technical of all. Rhythmically, the beat shifts from a feeling of 6/8 to 3/4 throughout, and should leave you breathless as it drives to the finish.

I owe a debt of gratitude to Charmaine Siagian and Richard Rejino for encouraging me to create this piano solo version. May it provide a rewarding musical experience for you.

Mona Rejino

Mona Rejino
May 2021

Contents

Impressions of New York

Impressions of New York

I. Strolling the Upper West Side

Mona Rejino

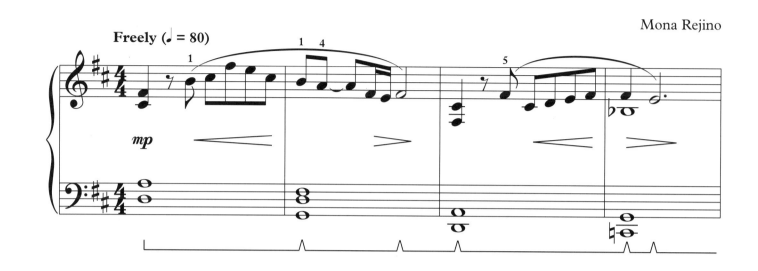

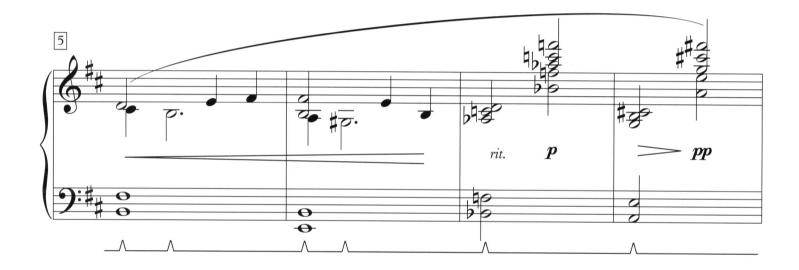

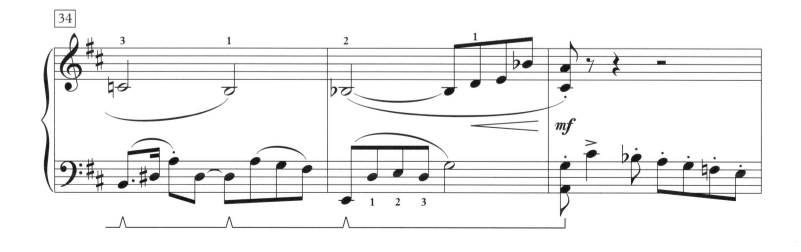

II. Midnight in Brooklyn

* *Tap fallboard with open hand.*

III. Grand Central Station

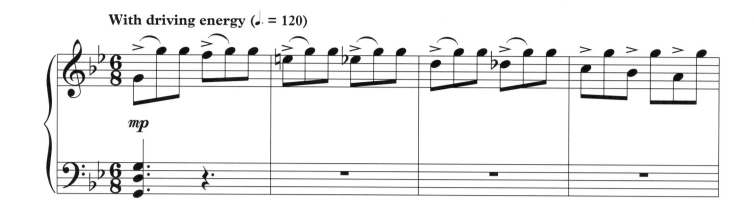

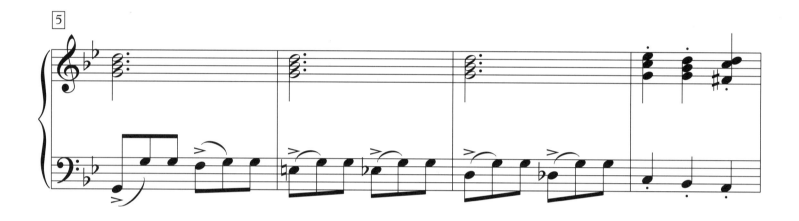

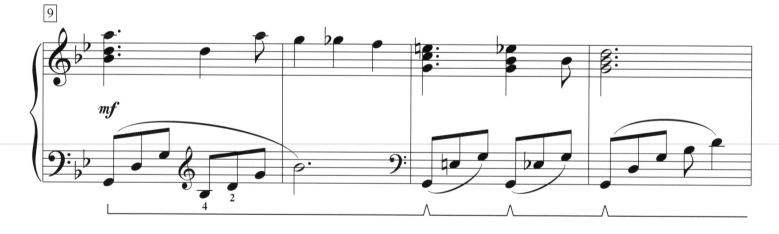

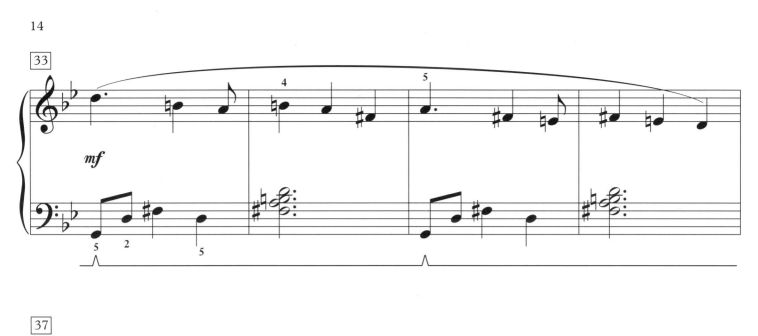

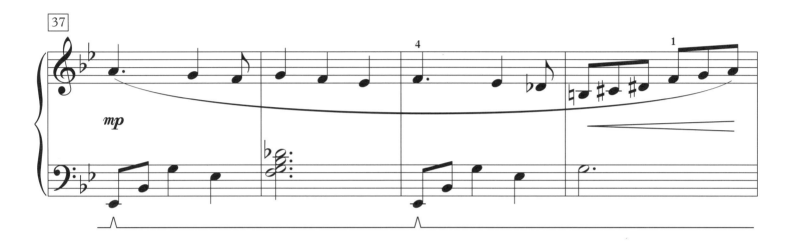

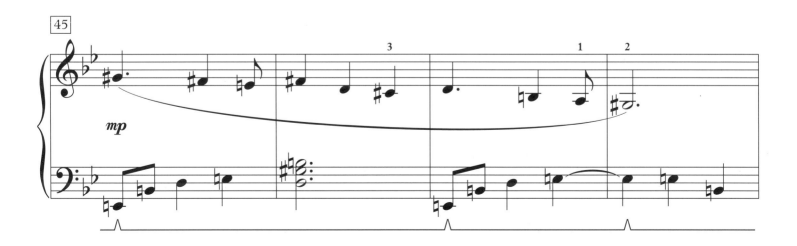